Table of Contents

Park Scavenger Hunt

Let's go on a hunt! Can we find these things at a park?

1 | tube shape -

2 | cold thing -

3 | water sound -

4 | flower smell -

5 | sweet taste -

6 | animal sound -

We have five **senses**. They can help find things.

I see with my eye.

I see a tube slide.

I feel with my hand.

I feel a cold swing.

I hear with my ear. I hear
a water fountain.

I smell with my nose.

I smell tulips.

I taste with my tongue.

I taste ice cream.

I hear with my ear. I hear
a bird **cooing**.

18

We found all 6 things!

Can you find them in your park? Happy hunting!

21

Make Your Own Scavenger Hunt

Decide Where to Go

Make a List of Things
You May Find

Add Senses to That List

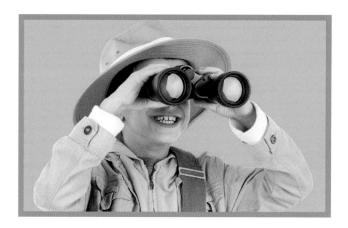

Find Your Things!

22

Glossary

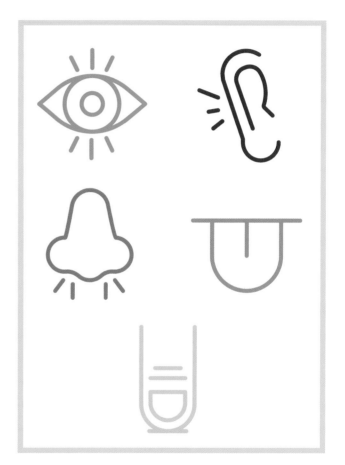

coo
the soft, muffled, and ongoing sound a pigeon makes.

sense
any of five ways to experience one's surroundings. The senses are sight, hearing, smell, taste, and touch.

Index

Abdo Kids
ONLINE
FREE! ONLINE MULTIMEDIA RESOURCES

Visit **abdokids.com**
to access crafts, games,
videos, and more!

Use Abdo Kids code

SMK1542

or scan this QR code!